The Proverbs 31 Woman:

31 Day Challenge Devotional

by Sharon Hamilton-Martin

I dedicate this book to my Heavenly Father and Creator, Jesus Christ, my Savior and Lord, and the Holy Spirit, my Helper, and Guide.

I dedicate this book to my husband, Keith Martin, Jr., and our sons Solomon Xavier and Zechariah Shawn-Benjamin, my motivation and inspiration for becoming a Proverbs 31 Woman.

In memory of my mother:
Erria B. Hamilton, for being a loving mother

In memory of my grandmothers:
"Muh Dear" & "Big Mama," wise, strong, loving women who held their families together

Contents

Preface

The Proverbs 31 Woman: 31 Day Challenge devotional was birthed out of morning meditations with God in December 2017. As I began to seek God about becoming the best woman of God that I can be for the upcoming year, the best wife that I can be, and the best mother that I can be...I realized that this was going to be **work** and that this was going to be **a challenge**. I'm not speaking of perfection, as in error-free, but as in maturing and discovering who God desires us to be. While pondering the challenge, I was reminded that most everyone was doing some challenge; so why not invite other women to join The Proverbs 31 Woman: 31 Day Challenge. A **challenge** is a call to action, and the purpose of a challenge is to help us become wiser and more substantial. A **devotional** is a brief worship encounter that brings us closer to God. I don't claim to be an expert at being The Proverbs 31 Woman, but it's my desire and reference point, and I'm striving to get there daily. Won't you take this journey with me!

The Proverbs 31 Woman:

31 Day Challenge Devotional

"Who can find a virtuous woman? For her price is far above rubies." -Proverbs 31:10

Day 1

T he Proverbs 31 Woman
31 Day Challenge Devotional

Proverbs 31:1 "The words of king Lemuel, the prophecy that his mother taught him."

Who was King Lemuel? Lemuel means devoted to God. King Lemuel was important enough to be recorded in the Bible. Notice that his mother **taught** him. King Lemuel's mother had to be a wise and influential woman to impart the wisdom she shared with her son, who became a high-ranking man of importance.

Challenge: Be wise women of God who can teach, influence, and impart godly wisdom to our sons and daughters. Mothers, grandmothers, stepmothers, godmothers, aunts, older sisters, and holy women of influence; let's raise godly kings for godly queens and godly queens for godly kings.

Day 2

⌒ↄ૦૮૦ↄ⌒

T he Proverbs 31 Woman
31 Day Challenge Devotional

Proverbs 31:2 "What, my son? and what, son of my womb? And what, the son of my vows?"

In this scripture, we witness a fully invested mother who is being accountable by embracing her child-rearing responsibilities and being hands-on in her approach.

Challenge: Let's be more hands-on. Let's be accountable. Let's be fully invested, and let's fully embrace our God-given responsibilities and assignments. Be blessed❤

Day 3

⚜

T he Proverbs 31 Woman
31 Day Challenge Devotional

Proverbs 31:3 "Give not thy strength unto women, Nor thy ways to that which destroyeth kings."

In this scripture, a command of caution is given about who and what to devote our strength to and a warning about our direction choices.

Challenge: Prioritize. Let's examine ourselves! To whom or what am I giving my strength, energy, and power? Does my way of doing things lead me to God's sovereign destiny in my life? Let's not give our strength, energy, and ability to persons or something which can detour us from God's sovereign destiny for our lives.

Day 4

The Proverbs 31 Woman
31 Day Challenge Devotional

Proverbs 31:4 *"It is* not for Kings, O Lemuel, *it is* not for kings to drink wine; Nor for princes strong drink;"

In this scripture, sobriety is advised! What is sobriety? In addition to the ability to think clearly, absent of the influence of alcohol and drugs, sobriety also means being sensible, being reasonable, being rational, having self-control, sanity, and having mental and emotional balance.

Challenge: Be sober-minded. As children of God, we are heirs of God and joint-heirs with Christ (Romans 8:16-17). This relationship makes us royalty through our confession, belief, and acceptance of Jesus and His work on the cross. Let's allow the Holy Spirit of God to influence our minds, thoughts, bodies, actions, spirits, and souls.

Day 5

The Proverbs 31 Woman
31 Day Challenge Devotional

Proverbs 31:5 "Lest they drink and forget the law, And pervert the judgment of any of the afflicted."

This scripture addresses the consequences of one's choices and actions. Will the choices and activities that we make cause us to forget the things of God or cause us to miss the mark?

Challenge: Be intentional in choosing a Christ-centered life! Watch it yield consequences that lead to blessings! Deuteronomy 30:19 says, "This day I call the heavens and earth as witnesses against you that I have set before you life and death, blessings and curses. Now choose life, so that you and your children may live."

Day 6

The Proverbs 31 Woman
31 Day Challenge Devotional

Proverbs 31:6 "Give strong drink unto him that is ready to perish, and wine unto those that be of heavy hearts."

This scripture paints a vivid picture of hopelessness. Think about it...drinking until one is ready to die sounds miserable, and a heavy heart represents sadness, grief, and depression.

Challenge: Keep Hope alive! Who and what is that Hope? Christ in you, The Hope of Glory! (Colossians 1:27)

Day 7

The Proverbs 31 Woman
31 Day Challenge Devotional

Proverbs 31:7 "Let him drink, and forget his poverty, And remember his misery no more."

In this scripture, we see a temporary means of escape for handling life's problems and circumstances.

Challenge: Seek God for solutions to life's problems and circumstances FIRST. He is waiting to help us. 1 Peter 5:7 says, "Casting all your care upon him; for he careth for you." and Proverbs 3:6 says, "In all thy ways acknowledge him, and he shall direct thy paths."

Day 8

 ⚜

T he Proverbs 31 Woman
31 Day Challenge Devotional

Proverbs 31:8 "Open thy mouth for the dumb In the cause of all such as are appointed to destruction."

In this scripture, there is a directive to be a voice for those who cannot speak for themselves or cannot defend themselves.

Challenge: Be a bold voice for righteousness. In Luke 12:12, Jesus spoke these words to His disciples, "For the Holy Ghost shall teach you in the same hour what ye ought to say." Are you a disciple? If so, you have the backing of the Holy Spirit.

Day 9

$\sim$

T he Proverbs 31 Woman
31 Day Challenge Devotional

Proverbs 31:9 "Open thy mouth, judge righteously, And plead the cause of the poor and needy."

In this scripture, instruction is given to help the righteous cause of the disadvantaged or those who lack necessary resources.

Challenge: Be an advocate that helps for a righteous cause. Has God been dealing with you about helping someone? Do you know anyone disadvantaged or lacks the necessary resources? 1 John 3:17 reminds us, "But whoso hath this world's good, and seeth his brother have need, and shutteth up his bowels of compassion from him, how dwelleth the love of God in him?" Now is the opportunity to be selfless by exercising a selfless deed!

Day 10

The Proverbs 31 Woman
31 Day Challenge Devotional

Proverbs 31:10 "Who can find a virtuous woman? For her price *is* far above rubies."

What does it mean to be virtuous? Virtuous means, but is not limited to, righteousness, moral excellence, purity, goodness, strength, dignity, integrity, respectability, decency, honor, and nobility, to name a few. This scripture implies that there is a shortage or scarcity of virtuous women. This scripture further says that a virtuous woman's worth exceeds and cannot be compared to monetary value.

Challenge: Strive to be virtuous and know your worth. We were created in the image of an All Mighty God. That makes us SOMEBODY special. Genesis 1:27 says, "So God created man in his own image, in the image of God created he him; male and female created he them."

Day 11

T he Proverbs 31 Woman
    31 Day Challenge Devotional

Proverbs 31:11 "The heart of her husband doth safely trust in her, So that he shall have no need of spoil."

This scripture exemplifies what genuine trust in a woman's marital relationship to her husband should entail. The heart refers to the inward parts (inner thoughts, inner feelings, inner desires. Trust means to have confidence in and to rely on or depend on. In essence, "safely trust" means to trust without reservations. In other words, the husband's wife is his confidant that he can talk to and not have to worry about what or who his wife may tell or how what he tells his wife may affect her attitude towards him or the situation after he shares his heart. Notice, according to this scripture, the husband will 'have no need of spoil.' Anything that **spoils** goes bad. As a result of the type of trust described in this scripture, the husband will have all he needs in his wife.

Challenge: Be trustworthy without reservations. Can someone share something personal with you, without fear that what they share with you will get out to others? The principle of being trustworthy can be extended to various godly relationships in our lives and should be practiced by us all.

Day 12

⁕

T
he Proverbs 31 Woman
31 Day Challenge Devotional

Proverbs 31:12 "She will do him good and not evil All the days of her life."

In this scripture, we see a marital example of a wife who beneficially adds to her husband's life. She operates with his best interest at heart and does right by him all the days of HER life. Wow! What dedication!

Challenge: Be a Beneficial Addition in life. Do we add or subtract from others? As children of God, Matthew 5:13 reminds us that we are the salt of the earth. Add your beneficial flavor to this Earth.

Day 13

⁓✦⁓

T he Proverbs 31 Woman
31 Day Challenge Devotional

Proverbs 31:13 "She seeketh wool, and flax, And worketh willingly with her hands."

In this scripture, we see an example of resourcefulness and productivity. Raw materials of that day were gathered and then processed. Note that the woman mentioned in this scripture worked willingly with her hands. The wool that she likely picked and processed would probably be used for fall/winter clothing, and the flax was likely processed into linen for spring/summer clothing.

Challenge: Be resourceful and productive. Let's ask ourselves," What will I produce with raw materials?" The scripture above reminds us of being good stewards. Colossians 3:23 (NKJV) reminds us, "And whatever you do, do it heartily, as to the Lord and not to men."

Day 14

The Proverbs 31 Woman
31 Day Challenge Devotional

Proverbs 31:14 "She is like the merchants' ships; she bringeth her food from afar."

In this scripture, we see an example of a woman who traveled to find a quality necessity....food.

Challenge: Stretch yourself spiritually! Let's ask ourselves, "How far am I willing to go in the Spirit to obtain the necessary spiritual food of God's Word?" In John 6:35a, Jesus reminds us that "I am the bread of life; whoever comes to me shall not hunger,"

Day 15

The Proverbs 31 Woman
31 Day Challenge Devotional

Proverbs 31:15 "She riseth also while it is yet night, And giveth meat to her household, and a portion to her maidens."

This scripture paints a clear picture of a woman, who is likely a wife and mother who gets up early and not only cooks for her family but gives them what they need, followed by providing her helpers with what they needed. Notice that even though this woman was prosperous enough to have maids, she still took the time to care for her family's personal needs first. This scripture teaches us an essential principle of the correlation between the diligence of getting up early, planning, and accomplishing tasks.

Challenge: Let's get up early. Let's receive spiritual "meat" for our households, including ourselves, to plan and accomplish the tasks at hand effectively. Study the scriptures, and we will find great things happened in the early morning hours. Proverbs 8:17 reminds us that those who seek Him early would find Him.

Day 16

⚜

T he Proverbs 31 Woman
    31 Day Challenge Devotional

Proverbs 31:16 "She considereth a field, and buyeth it: With the fruit of her hands she planteth a vineyard."

In this scripture, we see an example of how to invest and profit from that investment wisely.

Challenge: Let's make wise investments naturally and spiritually and watch it grow! Galatians 6:8 (NIV) reminds us, "Whoever sows to please their flesh, from the flesh will reap destruction; whoever sows to please the Spirit, from the Spirit will reap eternal life." Our first natural investment should be paying tithes and offerings. Malachi 3:10-11(NIV) says, "Bring the whole tithe into the storehouse, that there may be food in my house. Test me in this," says the Lord Almighty, "and see if I will not throw open the floodgates of heaven and pour out so much blessing that there will not be room enough to store it. I will prevent pests from devouring your crops, and the vines in your fields will not drop their fruit before it is ripe," says the Lord Almighty."

Day 17

T he Proverbs 31 Woman
    31 Day Challenge Devotional

Proverbs 31:17 "She girdeth her loins with strength, and strengtheneth her arms."

This scripture does not describe laziness. This scripture teaches us to condition ourselves by preparing, equipping, and readying ourselves for hard work.

Challenge: Let's push ourselves. Let's strength train in the Spirit! Jude 20 NKJV says, "But you, beloved, building yourselves up on your most holy faith, praying in the Holy Spirit."

Day 18

The Proverbs 31 Woman
31 Day Challenge Devotional

Proverbs 31:18 "She perceiveth that her merchandise *is* good: Her candle goeth not out by night."

In this scripture, we see an example of an excellent businesswoman. It's impressive that she was not satisfied with just having good merchandise or suitable substances. This woman continued to evolve and develop.

Challenge: Don't get stuck! Are you good at something? Why not become excellent at it?! **Don't let good be your stopping point.** Luke 2:52 says, "And Jesus kept increasing in wisdom and stature, and in favor with God and men." If Jesus, the Son of God, increased His wisdom and stature (reputation gained by ability or achievement); as Jesus' disciples, so should we!"

Day 19

⁓⦿⦿⦿⁓

T he Proverbs 31 Woman
31 Day Challenge Devotional

Proverbs 31:19 "She layeth her hands to the spindle, And her hands hold the distaff."

This scripture describes a woman making her thread and weaving or intertwining fabric to most likely make clothing. A simple truth: this woman used her hands to be a MAKER of something purposeful.

Challenge: Be a purposeful maker at home and in the community. Let's ask ourselves," Am I a purposeful maker, or am I a destroyer?" "Do I help to make things better or worse?" Anytime something is made, it is another way of saying built. Proverbs 14:1 (NIV) says it best; "The wise woman builds her house, but with her own hands the foolish one tears hers down." Be blessed❣

Day 20

The Proverbs 31 Woman
31 Day Challenge Devotional

Proverbs 31:20 "She stretcheth out her hand to the poor; Yea, she reacheth forth her hands to the needy."

In this scripture, we see an example of an unselfish and concerned individual taking action by ministering to others' needs. We are called to be the extended hands of God.

Challenge: Be the extended hands that God can use to minister to the needs of others. Let's ask God, "Lord, how can I minister to the needs of others?" The Greek definition of the word minister is 'a waiter, servant; anyone who performs any service, an administrator.' We do not have to have the title of a minister to minister. Matthew 25:35a, 40 (NIV) says, "For I was hungry, and you gave me something to eat, I was thirsty, and you gave me something to drink...The King will reply, 'Truly I tell you, whatever you did for one of the least of these brothers and sisters of mine, you did for me.'" Be Blessed♥

Day 21

Day 21

The Proverbs 31 Woman
31 Day Challenge Devotional

Proverbs 31:21 "She is not afraid of the snow for her household: For all her household are clothed with scarlet."

In this scripture, we see an example of preparation and properly covering others for the season at hand. Although this scripture does not say winter season, it does imply it. Winter tends to be the coldest, slowest and harshest time of the seasons. Scarlet is a fine luxury wool fabric used particularly for winter clothing because it preserves warmth. In the Old Testament, scarlet pointed to Jesus' Blood sacrifice on the cross.

Challenge: Prepare by being covered and protected. Let's ask ourselves, "Am I prepared? Am I covered and protected?" The Blood of Jesus covers and protects us in every season of life, especially in our lives' cold and winter seasons. When we prepare, and when we are covered and protected, we can cause our household to be covered. Exodus 12:13a (NIV) reminds us, "The blood will be a sign for you on the houses where you are, and when I see the blood, I will pass over you..." Be Blessed.❣

Day 22

⁓ ❧✦❧ ⁓

T he Proverbs 31 Woman
31 Day Challenge Devotional

Proverbs 31:22 "She maketh herself coverings of tapestry; Her clothing *is* silk and purple."

In this scripture, we see an example of an individual who did not forget to cover and take care of herself. Silk represented luxury. Purple represented royalty, wealth, or prosperity.

Challenge: Don't forget the importance of self-care. We cannot effectively help others if we are not adequately covered and have not taken the time to care for ourselves properly. We belong to God. Let's represent Him well. Let's take care of ourselves both naturally and spiritually. Ephesians 5:29-30 (NIV) says, "After all, no one ever hated their own body, but they feed and care for their body, just as Christ does the church- for we are members of His Body."

Day 23

The Proverbs 31 Woman
31 Day Challenge Devotional

Proverbs 31:23 "Her husband is known in the gates, When he sitteth among the elders of the land."

This scripture reveals the reward of this woman's private support of her spouse. Because of the greatness of who she was, her husband benefitted. He was known and held a position of influence. As the saying goes, "behind every great man is a greater woman."

Challenge: Be supportive of others and watch God bless you and those connected to you.

Day 24

The Proverbs 31 Woman
31 Day Challenge Devotional

Proverbs 31:24 "She maketh fine linen, and selleth it; And delivereth girdles unto the merchant."

In this scripture, we see that this woman was a manufacturer with good business insight. She supplied the demands.

Challenge: Supply the demand for the Kingdom of God! God has put something in each of us both naturally and spiritually that others need. It's time to pay up!!! Let's ask ourselves, "What gifts or talents have the Heavenly Father supplied me with? Am I meeting Heaven's demands? Ephesians 2:10 (NIV) says, "For we are God's handiwork, created in Christ Jesus to do good works, which God prepared in advance for us to do."

Day 25

The Proverbs 31 Woman
31 Day Challenge Devotional

Proverbs 31:25 "Strength and honour *are* her clothing; And she shall rejoice in time to come."

In this scripture, there is mention of this woman being clothed or covered with strength and honor. As a result, she was able to celebrate the future.

Challenge: Let God cover you! Psalms 46:1 says, "God is our refuge and strength, an ever-present help in trouble." and Proverbs 21:21 (NIV) tells us, "Whoever pursues righteousness and love finds life, prosperity and honor." With God's covering of strength and honor, we can celebrate the future.

Day 26

~~~

The Proverbs 31 Woman
31 Day Challenge Devotional

Proverbs 31:26 "She openeth her mouth with wisdom; And in her tongue *is* the law of kindness."

In this scripture, we see an example of how to speak. Notice wisdom is used and kindness. Wisdom can involve using sound judgment, knowledge, and experience. Godly wisdom involves all of the above, with the leading, insight, correct decision making, and discernment of the Holy Spirit. Why kindness? Because loving kindness draws, and it can be a reflection of God. It matters: what we say, how we say it, and where we say it!

Challenge: Let's watch our language by using wisdom when we speak. In listening to ourselves and others' language, it clarifies what's going on inside of us. Words are powerful, and scripture reminds us that death and life can be found in the power of the tongue (Proverbs 18:21). We must practice speaking life to ourselves and others that are around us.❦

Day 27

⁓⌇⁓

The Proverbs 31 Woman
31 Day Challenge Devotional

Proverbs 31:27 "She looketh well to the ways of her household, And eateth not the bread of idleness."

Notice that in this scripture, we see an example of a proactive individual. This woman was watchful and attentive to her home's needs and the conduct and activities. Secondly, notice that this woman was not lazy or slothful. In fact, "She was on it! She was ahead of the curve!" Her eyes and ears were open, and she was at work meeting the needs of her household.

Challenge: Be proactive and be ahead of the curve! Whether single, single with children, or married, God desires to keep us in the know. As it relates to the state of our spiritual house (our body) and natural house and the natural household needs and the spiritual needs of our household (children, spouse) this is why God gave us the gift of His Holy Spirit. His Holy Spirit keeps us informed and empowers us (Acts 1:8) to take necessary actions. John 16:31 (NIV) says, "But when he, the Spirit of truth, comes, he will guide you into all the truth. He will not speak on his own; he will speak only what he hears, and he will tell you what is yet to come." Humanly, we will not know everything that our household needs naturally or spiritually, but the Holy Spirit sees and hears everything about everyone and knows what is required. If we seek The Holy Spirit, there is absolutely nothing that He will not reveal to us!

Day 28

T he Proverbs 31 Woman
31 Day Challenge Devotional

Proverbs 31:28 "Her children arise up, and call her blessed; Her husband *also*, and he praiseth her."

In this scripture, we witness the reward of a devoted mother and wife to her family. Her children and her husband honored her and spoke well of her.

Challenge: Be devoted. It has its benefits. Galatians 6:9 (NIV) says, "Let us not become weary in doing good, for at the proper time we will reap a harvest if we do not give up."

Day 29

The Proverbs 31 Woman
31 Day Challenge Devotional

Proverbs 31:29 "Many daughters have done virtuously, But thou excellest them all."

In this scripture, we see an example of moral excellence. In essence, this woman was the best among other morally good women. It wasn't enough for her to be mediocre or have the attitude that good enough will do!

Challenge: Let's strive to have a spirit of excellence in all that we do. In Daniel 6:3, Daniel was recorded as having an excellent spirit. "Then this Daniel was preferred above the presidents and princes, because an excellent spirit [was] in him; and the king thought to set him over the whole realm." We serve an excellent God!!! Let's let excellence be our goal.❣

Day 30

‿❧⚬❦⚬❧‿

The Proverbs 31 Woman
31 Day Challenge Devotional

Proverbs 31:30 "Favour *is* deceitful, and beauty *is* vain: *But* a woman *that* feareth the LORD, she shall be praised."

This scripture gets to the heart of the matter by putting things in perspective. The scripture noted that fearing or reverencing and honoring God caused this woman to shine and be celebrated. This scripture also reminded us that favor or charm could be deceiving, and outer beauty is superficial and can fade away. This scripture may also imply that the woman described in this chapter may not have been considered the most outwardly attractive of women, but her inner beauty mattered the most.

Challenge: Be beautiful from the inside out! Psalms 149:4 reminds us, "For the LORD taketh pleasure in his people: he will beautify the meek with salvation."

Day 31

The Proverbs 31 Woman
31 Day Challenge Devotional

Proverbs 31:31 "Give her of the fruit of her hands; And let her own works praise her in the gates."

In this scripture, a command is given for this woman to be rewarded and publicly recognized for all of her works. God is just that type of God! When we do things with a pure heart and pure motives, God takes notice, and so do others, and God will command that others recognize you. Your labor in the Lord is never in vain (1 Cor. 15:58b).

Challenge: Keep working with a pure heart and pure motives! Romans 2:6 (NIV) reminds us of this, "God "will repay each person according to what they have done."❤

Conclusion

ooray! You made it to the end of this challenge. You answered the call to action, and now you are stronger and wiser for it.

It is my prayer that this devotional has sparked the fire of spiritual growth in each of you. I pray that each woman who reads this devotional will discover the Proverbs 31 Woman within her that God designed her to be. May the Holy Spirit add more wisdom, knowledge, and understanding of these scriptures through the depth of the Word in Jesus' Name. Amen.

About the Author

Sharon Hamilton-Martin is a wife, mother, and disciple of Jesus Christ who is passionate about helping, encouraging, empowering, teaching, and reaching others. Sharon enjoys traveling, meeting others, and learning new things. She received a Bachelor of Science degree in Educational Psychology with a minor in Corrections. Sharon received a Master of Science degree in Counselor Education, with a specialty in Community Counseling. She has worked in the mental health profession for over 22 years.